HOW TO USE YOUR TIME WISELY

This *No Nonsense Guide* shows you

★ How to accomplish more

★ The art of meeting deadlines

★ How to stop procrastinating

★ All you need to know to become a Time Management P•R•O

★ How to put the NoNonsense G•O•L•D principle to work for you

THE NO NONSENSE LIBRARY

NO NONSENSE FINANCIAL GUIDES

How to Finance Your Child's College Education
How to Use Credit and Credit Cards, Revised Edition
• *Understanding Tax-Exempt Bonds, Revised Edition*
Understanding Money Market Funds, Revised Edition
Understanding Mutual Funds, Revised Edition
• *Understanding IRA's*
Understanding Common Stocks, Revised Edition
Understanding Treasury Bills and Other U.S. Government Securities, Revised Edition
• *Understanding the Stock Market, Revised Edition*
Understanding Stock Options and Futures Markets, Revised Edition
How to Choose a Discount Stockbroker, Revised Edition
• *How to Make Personal Financial Planning Work for You*
How to Plan and Invest for Your Retirement
The New Tax Law and What It Means to You

NO NONSENSE REAL ESTATE GUIDES

Understanding Condominiums and Co-ops, Revised Edition
• *Understanding Buying and Selling a House, Revised Edition*
• *Understanding Mortgages and Home Equity Loans, Revised Edition*
Refinancing Your Mortgage, Revised Edition

NO NONSENSE LEGAL GUIDES

Understanding Estate Planning and Wills, Revised Edition
How to Choose A Lawyer

NO NONSENSE CAREER GUIDES

• *How to Use Your Time Wisely* ✓
• *Managing People: At Work, At Home*

NO NONSENSE SUCCESS GUIDES

NO NONSENSE HEALTH GUIDES

NO NONSENSE COOKING GUIDES

NO NONSENSE WINE GUIDES

HOW TO USE YOUR TIME WISELY

Phyllis C. Kaufman
& Arnold Corrigan

LONGMEADOW PRESS

How to Use Your Time Wisely

Production services by William S. Konecky Associates, New York.

Published 1987 by Longmeadow Press, 201 High Ridge Road, Stamford, Connecticut 06904.

No Nonsense Career Guide is a trademark controlled by Longmeadow Press.

ISBN: 0-681-40136-2

Printed in the United States of America

0 9 8 7 6 5 4 3 2 1

TO

Eva and Sergio Franchi

with love

CONTENTS

Introduction   The G∗O∗L∗D Principle   ix

Part I   Go for the G∗O∗L∗D

1. Setting Goals   3
2. Goals and Time   5
3. Organizing Priorities   10
4. "I've Got a Little List"   15
5. Scheduling Your Day—Your Biological Clock   19
6. Calendars   22
7. Do It Now!   26
8. Goals Revisited   27

Part II   Coping With Paper

9. Toss It! File It! Move It!   35
10. The Art of Filing   38
11. Dealing with Paper at the Office   44
12. Dealing with Paper at Home   46

Part III   Dealing with Interruptions and Schedule-Breakers

13. The Telephone and Uninvited Visitors   53
14. Coping With Emergencies and Crises   58
15. Meetings   60

Part IV   How to Avoid Being Overwhelmed

16. Saying No   65
17. When and How Not to be Perfect   68
18. Panic   70

Part V   Time Wasters

19. Nine No Nonsense Time Wasters and
    their Cures   77
20. Procrastination—Causes and Cures   81

Part VI   Organizing for Maximum Efficiency

21. A Place For Everything and Everything
    in its Place   87
22. Your Desk   90
23. Your Kitchen   93
24. Your Closets   96

Conclusion   Be a Time Management P*R*O   97
Index   100

INTRODUCTION
THE G*O*L*D PRINCIPLE

> You can ask me for anything you like, except time.
> Napoleon Bonaparte

There is never enough time. Once a second is gone, it can never be recaptured. While we can accumulate other things—money, clothes, cars, power—we cannot accumulate more time. No matter what we do, no matter how hard we work, and no matter how conscientious we are, each of us has only a finite amount of time to use and enjoy.

So managing your time—making the most of this rare and wonderful gift—is essential to living your life the way you want to live it.

G*O*L*D

What is the G*O*L*D Principle? It is a method of taking control of your time. By applying the G*O*L*D Principle to your everyday chores as well as your long-range planning, you can become better organized, more productive, and more successful in doing the things you want to do.

The G*O*L*D Principle stands for four simple steps that are your key to managing your time wisely and effectively:

1. Setting your *Goals* (for the day, the year, and beyond).
2. *Organizing* your priorities and planning how to achieve your goals.
3. *Listing* the things you will do on a given day (and sometimes for longer periods).
4. And finally—*Do It Now!* The time has come to begin.

PART I
GO FOR
THE G*O*L*D

PART I

1 · SETTING GOALS

Setting Goals is the first step in the G•O•L•D Principle, and the first key to time management.

From early childhood, we are asked to think about goals. Do you remember the question, "What do you want to be when you grow up?" And do you remember the answer? This question, often asked half-jokingly of a young child, becomes a serious matter as the child grows older and has to begin choosing an educational path. Many children, as they mature, take the question to heart and think hard and seriously about it.

Yet, if you ask many adults the same question, phrased just a little differently—What do you want to do with the rest of your life?—the types of response vary widely. Some have clear, well-articulated plans stretching far into the future. Others have not arrived at any clear goals. Still others have never taken the time to think about it. Some seem to be wandering aimlessly, "going with the flow."

Why Set Goals?

Some people may be content to "go with the flow" and to accept whatever may arrive. But most of us have goals we would like to reach—even if we are sometimes afraid to admit our goals because of lack of confidence or fear of disappointment. Thinking clearly about these goals is an essential step toward taking control of your time and your life. If your goals usually don't get past the daydream stage, you will find that articulating them and writing them down will make you come to grips with your hopes and desires and will open the way to making at least some of those desires become realities.

It's easy to see why setting goals is the first step in the G•O•L•D Principle. You can't organize your time effectively unless you are clear about what you are trying to do. Or, to put it differently—if you don't know where you are going, you are bound to waste time getting there.

2 · GOALS AND TIME

Goals come in all shapes and sizes. In particular, as you think about your goals, you will find that they have different time frames. You will have some very long-term goals, others that might be called mid-range, others that are shorter-term, and still others that have to be accomplished in the next day or week and that can be labeled immediate.

Length of Goals

Just how these different time frames break down into actual months and years will vary greatly depending on individual situations and, in particular, on age. An 18-year-old whose long-term goal is to become a skilled surgeon faces more than 12 years of mid-range goals—college, medical school, and residency. On the other hand, a person 64 years old who plans to retire at 65 is likely to have a cluster of mid-range goals for the next year or year and a half, centered around preparing and planning for retirement. As you grow older, the time periods naturally become compressed.

Two Types of Goals

Your mid-range goals can be of two types—those that relate to accomplishing your long-range goals, and those that are independent goals in themselves. Similarly, your short-term goals will include those that take you toward mid-range and longer objectives, and those that are self-contained.

The shortest-term goals, which we have labeled "immediate," are largely those constantly changing items that you have to do on an "as required by your daily life" basis. They include the report your boss needs by Wednesday at 2:00 P.M., shopping for toothpaste, preparing dinner for relatives, etc. Trivial or not, these are goals you want to reach as efficiently as possible. The requirements of your job, family situations, and the burdens of daily life will probably cause you to update your immediate goal list daily.

Let's Begin

Ultimately, your shorter-term goals are necessarily intertwined with your longer-term goals. But for simplicity and clarity, we will begin your education in time management by working with a one-year period—short enough to be manageable, but long enough so that some of your longer-term plans and desires will undoubtedly enter in. We will return to the subject of longer-term goals in Chapter 8.

Start with a clean sheet of paper, a pencil, and absolute quiet. Take the next 10 minutes (at least) to think about your desires and objectives for the coming 12 months. Don't limit yourself, and don't be afraid to think about goals that seem difficult or impractical. The first step is to let your thoughts run free so that you can recognize your own desires and objectives. Separating the practical from the impractical will come later.

After taking at least ten minutes, write your goals for the next year on the paper. Note them briefly, without excessive verbiage, and as clearly as possible. At first, they don't have to be in any particular order. Wherever possible, express your goals in words that describe what *you* can do. Don't be hesitant; remember that these are *your* goals, and no one else need share them with you.

Now break the list down into time segments. To accomplish those goals in a year, what goals should you set yourself for the first month, three months, six months, and nine months? Here are some examples of how your next list might be set up:

Mati is a homemaker. She has spent the last 20 years raising two children. During almost all of that time, her husband, daughter and son have been her first priority, and she has been rewarded with two healthy, intelligent, energetic children. Her youngest child will start college in the fall, and Mati wants to reenter the job market. Her long-range goal is to work in real estate, which she thinks will prove satisfying and monetarily rewarding.

Mati's 12-month goal is to find a job in real estate. Her shorter-term goals look like this:

1-month goals:

1. Research the requirements for a real estate license.
2. Enroll in a real estate course.
3. Explore networking groups for women trying to reenter the job market. Attend at least one meeting.

3-month goals:

1. Attend real estate classes.
2. Subscribe to and regularly read real estate publications.

6-month goals:

1. Continue studying for real estate examination.
2. Attend seminars and other meetings to become acquainted with members of the real estate community.

9-month goals:

1. Continue studying for real estate examination. Devote at least 3 hours a day to exam preparation.
2. Complete all paperwork for real estate license.
3. Prepare resumé for job hunting.
4. Obtain interviews with real estate firms.

12-month goals:

1. Take and pass real estate examination. Obtain real estate license.
2. Continue job hunting. Obtain a job with a real estate firm.

As you can see, Mati has broken down her goals very effectively into practical, meaningful time frames. By setting her goals carefully, she has already made important headway toward the critical step of setting time priorities, which we will discuss in Chapter 3.

Another Example

We'd also like you to meet Harry. At age 72, Harry recently sold his business and retired. He now wants to change his lifestyle and do what he always wanted to do—attend classes at local colleges, go to the theatre and concerts, and play golf. Harry's ambitious but practical 12-month goal is to change his life to make the most of his retirement. His short-term goals look like this:

1-month goals:

1. Obtain catalogues from area colleges.
2. Explore the courses and other activities available to Senior Citizens in his area.
3. Investigate subscription series to theatre and concerts.
4. Investigate free and low-price theatre and concert events at local universities, music schools, etc.
5. Explore the various golf courses in the area.

3-month goals:

1. Join a golf club.
2. Find golf partners and set up at least two regular weekly games.
3. Enroll in at least one college course.
4. Attend at least three lectures.
5. Join at least two museums.
6. Purchase at least one subscription series to plays or concerts.

6-month goals:

1. Begin attending regular classes.
2. Set aside at least one and one-half hours each day for course study.
3. Play golf at least twice each week, weather permitting.
4. Attend concerts at least twice a month and theatre at least once a month.

12-month goals:

1. Solidifying new routine of classes, study, theatre and concert events, meeting friends, and golf.

2. Consider which parts of the routine are most satisfying.
3. Set revised goals for the following year.
4. Play better golf.

Keeping Goals in Mind

You should always try to keep your longer-term (in this case, one year) goals in mind. You might want to make a small card listing your goals to carry in your wallet (one of your authors does). Look at it whenever you feel you lack direction or are overwhelmed. Proper use of this card will result in a clearer sense of your priorities (see Chapter 3) at times of confusion. It will also result in one very tattered piece of paper by December 31. Then, on January 1, you can throw away last year's card and start fresh.

Go for the G*O*L*D

Now is the time for you to take that piece of paper and quietly think about your goals for the next year. What do you want to accomplish? Write down your goals and then arrange them in a reasonable time sequence.

If you have listed and arranged your goals as carefully as we saw done above by Mati and Harry, you are now ready to begin moving toward those goals. To use your time wisely, the next step is to learn how to set and maintain priorities.

3 · ORGANIZING PRIORITIES

You have set your goals. The most important single step in reaching those goals is learning how to O•rganize Priorities. This is the "O" in the G•O•L•D Principle.

The Relationship Between Goals and Priorities

Let's step back for a moment and look at the whole problem. Most of us can learn to sit down, take time out, and work out a careful list of our goals, as we discussed in Chapter 2. But most of us—let's face it—have trouble in handling our priorities so that we *reach* the goals successfully.

This is what time management is all about. It's not easy to find time to do all the things you want to do. And it's not easy to manage your time so that all the *important* things get done when they should be done. You will reach your goals only if you *organize* your time—which means that you must Organize Priorities.

Most of your time is spent on tasks which are a step toward some goal. Very simply, the tasks which go the furthest toward accomplishing your most important goals are the tasks you must establish as having the highest priority.

No Nonsense Rule: Not all tasks are created equal.

Priorities and Rewards

To assign priorities, you must think very hard about the "reward" or "payoff" that you expect to result from the completion of a particular task. Rewards can come in many forms. They can be monetary—a raise or a promotion to a better-paying job. They can be physical—the feeling of well-being after you complete a three-mile run. Often the reward involves recognition by others—approval by your boss, for example, if you have completed a difficult assignment quickly and well. Sometimes there is no external recognition, and the reward is purely internal—your own satisfaction at having completed a task which you know is basically important or which has moved you closer to the accomplishment of your long-range goals.

High Priority/High Reward

So prior to beginning a task, carefully analyze its reward potential. Give high priority to high-reward items. High-reward items should take up more of your time and should be completed first. We find that it is invariably better to do a little work on a high priority item than a lot of work on one of lower priority. If you are about to spend a substantial amount of time on a low-priority item, rethink your motives and priorities carefully.

By analyzing and organizing your priorities so that you work the hardest and longest on items of highest priority, you will also be constantly rethinking and redirecting yourself toward your goals. And you may find, on reconsideration, that certain low-priority tasks can be abandoned entirely, or perhaps shifted to someone else.

Seeing the Big Picture

Your long-range goals (in the present case, 12 months) are the "big picture." Keep this big picture in mind when organizing your daily and weekly activities.

Granted, little interruptions or emergencies may get you off the track temporarily, but by keeping the big picture in mind, you will never let these interruptions permanently sidetrack you.

Assigning Priorities

How do you assign specific priorities? Every case is different, but one rule that always applies is to think before you act. Don't thoughtlessly get involved in a time-consuming task that could have been avoided.

There are many ways of analyzing the relative merits

of various projects. One is to judge based on the requester. A seemingly minor request from your biggest client may hold a far greater ultimate reward, in terms of your income and future, than a large assignment from a smaller client who regularly fails to pay his/her bills.

You can actually assign a priority number to a task, with a one for the most productive and a ten for the least. We suggest doing this for a month or so, until it becomes a habit.

An Example

Marvin is a young attorney working in a large law firm. His 12-month goal is to become a partner in the firm. He is bogged down with many pressing matters when one of the senior partners brings him a small problem from Mr. Rose, one of the firm's most important clients. While the matter is one that could easily be handled by a less-experienced attorney, Marvin takes a moment to rethink his day and reprioritize.

Granted, Marvin has many important tasks to handle for other clients, but (a) he wants to impress the senior partner and (b) he knows that Mr. Rose is of the utmost importance to the firm. Rose's problem is not complex, and under other circumstances Marvin would probably delegate it to a younger associate. But because Mr. Rose and the senior partner will appreciate his personal attention, the rewards for doing the job himself are great. So Marvin assigns a number one priority to the task.

But what about the day's other priorities? Marvin looks at the other pressing matters before him. He planned to complete four specific items today. One of them, however, a rather time-consuming matter for Mr. Doyle, could be assigned a lower priority number. You see, Mr. Doyle does not pay his bills promptly, if at all, and probably gives the firm as much aggravation as profit. So Marvin's solution, based on his 12-month goal of becoming a partner of the firm, is to substitute the minor-but-high-reward Rose matter for the major-but-low-reward Doyle matter. In this way, Marvin has organized his priorities to maximize his rewards. And he has not made the mistake of trying to complete five jobs in a day that only has room for four.

Goal Visualization

Setting priorities and sticking to them is by no means easy. Often the choices and efforts required are difficult. But if you are serious about reaching your goals, you can learn to make these choices effectively.

Part of the trick is to keep your eye on the *goal*, on the ultimate reward, so that you don't get stopped or side-tracked by the tasks that lie on the way.

Here's an exercise you might want to try. Choose one of your goals. Visualize it. Try to feel how good it will be once you have achieved it.

Next, visualize all of the steps you must take to achieve that goal. If certain steps seem too difficult, try to break them down in your mind into more manageable pieces.

Now try to see your goal as if it were on the other side of a fast-moving river, with dangerous currents and white water. When you look closely at the river, you see that there are stones—some slippery, some dry, some jagged, and some flat. When you look closer still, you see that these stones form a path across the river.

You start across slowly, getting your footing, avoiding the slippery and jagged rocks. As you get further across the river, you are able to see the stones more clearly and to choose the best and quickest path toward the other side.

Reaching your goals has much in common with crossing a river. You must choose the rocks with the highest reward—those that lead you swiftly to the other side. All other rocks must be avoided or stepped over quickly. They are distractions that will only slow you down in reaching your reward.

We repeat that you must think before you act. Look at each task as it applies to your goals. If it is integral to a goal, then mark it as a high priority item for swift completion. If you find that one part of the task is too difficult, break it down into smaller parts. If a job seems important, but is a distraction from your goal, you must choose carefully whether or not to do it and, if you do it, how much time (priority) to allocate.

When Emotions Deserve Priority

There will be activities on your list that give you a low payoff in terms of achieving your long-range goals, but a high payoff emotionally. These include time spent with family, caring for children and relatives, helping friends, charity work, etc. High emotional payoff is as important to each of us as any other goal orientation. Or, to put it differently, these activities may take you toward goals that usually don't appear on any list—goals in personal fulfillment and personal relationships. You have every right to rank these emotionally gratifying tasks as equal to any others; how you balance them must remain a matter for your individual judgment.

Too Much to Do, Too Little Time

It sometimes happens that you cannot do all the things you need to do. Don't panic. Instead, be clearheaded and ruthless. The first step is to eliminate all unnecessary projects by delegating them to others.

What if you are not in a position to delegate? Then you must recognize your inability to do everything and either (a) tell your boss (or the requester) of your dilemma and mutually reschedule your priorities or (b) accept the reality that some things simply will not get done. In the latter case, make sure that the items which do not get done are those of lower priority/lower reward.

As we said, this is the time to be ruthless. Only do the projects of the highest-priority/reward quotient. And remember our rule—not all tasks are created equal. For a further discussion on this topic, see Part IV—How to Avoid Being Overwhelmed.

4 · "I'VE GOT A LITTLE LIST"

How can you remember the things you have to do, the things you want to do, and your goals, while at the same time coping with everyday life? There is a simple way—to make a list. L·isting your priorities and what you want to accomplish is the third element, the "L," in the G·O·L·D Principle.

Listing Your Long-Term Goals

As we mentioned in Chapter 2, it may be a good idea to list your longer-term goals (for now, 12 months) on a small card and carry it with you in your wallet or purse. There are many times during a year when one can become overwhelmed and not know in what direction to turn. Having this overview list to refer to can help clear your thinking and set you on the right course.

Monthly List

You should reevaluate your handling of priorities on a regular basis. A good idea is to take 15 minutes the first of every month to analyze what you have accomplished toward your goals in the last month and what you hope to do this month.

You may find that you want to make this review of goals more or less often than monthly. The choice is yours. Throughout this book, we offer suggestions in forms that have worked for us. We suggest that you try them, and then change or refine the details in order to make the system work for you.

What to List

Keeping your long- and mid-range goals in mind, look at the coming month and see what you can do in the month to advance your objectives. List all the tasks you hope to accomplish. The first draft of the list doesn't have to be in any particular order.

Prioritize!

Now, rank each of the listed items in terms of reward. (See Chapter 3.) High-reward items should receive a higher priority than low-payoff ones. Number all the items on your list by priority, starting with the highest priority as number one.

Your Daily List

Your long-range goals aren't the only things you have to think about each day. There are daily job and family responsibilities as well as the necessities of living, such as doing the laundry and shopping for groceries. A daily, or "today" list helps you set priorities, ensures that the top-priority items get done, helps you complete other items as well, and lets you avoid that terrible feeling that you have been "spinning your wheels" all day.

Some people prefer to organize their daily list the first thing in the morning. Others do it the night before. In any case, don't trust your memory. The list has to be written down, on a piece of paper compact enough for you to carry with you for reference throughout the day.

Try to be specific and break each item into its component parts. Don't list "make phone calls." Rather list:

1. Call Beth.
2. Return Bebe's call.
3. Call Stu.
4. Work on new job resumé.
5. Buy fish, broccoli, eggs, and flour for dinner.
6. Make carrot cake.

We recommend that while making out your daily list, you refer briefly to your monthly priorities list. Does the day's schedule help you toward your major objectives? Or have you let yourself be distracted by trivia and low-priority items? Be tough on yourself. Now is the time to get back on the track.

Be Realistic

Try not to overschedule yourself each day. You might try ranking your items by priority and then adding a second lower-priority list to be worked on if you have extra time.

Separate lists can serve other functions. For example, if you need toothpaste and deodorant, you might have a separate "drugstore" list. On the first day that you find yourself near a drugstore, you could run in and buy the items on your list, without having taken the time to make a special trip.

Prioritize According to Time and Location

Always try to keep time and location constraints in mind when organizing your daily lists. Let's say that you need to visit a particular department store, a nearby bank and the post office. The store doesn't open until 10:00 A.M., the bank gets crowded by 10:30, and the post office has long lines after 9:45. An efficient schedule might take you to the post office at 9:30 A.M., the bank at 9:45, and let you arrive just after opening at the department store.

If you need to run an errand that involves a long walk, consider scheduling it at lunchtime or after work, when you may welcome the walk for relaxation. Or, if you want to do some summer gardening, it is best scheduled early or late in the day when the sun is not as strong.

Counting the Hours

If you find that you get less done in a day than you think you should, consider setting time limits for each task on your daily list. If you are trying to fit too many tasks into the day, this will help you spot the problem quickly—the numbers will add up to more total time than you actually have in the day. On the other hand, if the times seem reasonable but you find yourself falling behind schedule, there are two likely explanations: either you have underestimated the time needed for particular tasks (many of us are guilty of this kind of overoptimism), or you have let yourself be lured into spending too much time on nonessentials (browsing in the supermarket aisles, doing the daily crossword puzzle, etc.). Once you find the source of the problem, you can plan your days more realistically and successfully.

5 · SCHEDULING YOUR DAY—YOUR BIOLOGICAL CLOCK

Are you a morning or an evening person? Are you at your peak early in the day or after the sun sets?

The Morning Majority

The great majority of people tend to be "morning people"— that is, they are at their most productive and thoughtful early in the day, sometime between the hours of 6:00 A.M. and noon. There are many, however, who seem to be unable to act with vigor before noon and who really don't reach their stride until after 5:00 P.M. or even later at night.

Which are You?

In order to find the prime hours of your own biological clock, we suggest that you do this simple test. Over the next few days, try doing complicated tasks at various times of the day. A difficult crossword puzzle is ideal. Try the puzzle when you first get up, at about 10:00 A.M., at noon, 2:00 P.M., 4:00 P.M., just before and after dinner, and again at about 10:00 P.M. When did you find the puzzle the easiest? Did more words come to you early or later in the day?

The Evening Person

As we noted, most of us are morning people. But if you find that you are sluggish early in the day, begin picking up steam by the afternoon, and go into full gear in the evening, you are probably an evening person.

Being an evening person in our society can be difficult, because your most productive hours are not those you spend at work. But if you are a person whose goals are other than those of your present job, your biological clock may be a real blessing. It will allow you to do your day job at your regular pace, while reserving your most productive hours for your personal goals.

Using Your Biological Clock

By scheduling your day according to your biological clock, you can maximize your efficiency. Very simply, you should work on your most complicated and highest-priority projects during your most productive hours.

For example, let's say that you are a morning person and that your prime goal is to become a registered nurse. You work all day as a laboratory technician and take courses at night toward your nursing degree. As a morning person, it takes all your concentration to stay alert for these evening courses. But your morningness will allow you to get up early (though you may hate the thought of doing it), do your studying and prepare for class before going to work. In class, despite your fatigue, take as many notes as possible, even though you don't fully absorb what the professor is saying. The next morning, you can reread your notes when your mind is clearest.

Maximizing High-Productivity Time

By scheduling your high-priority items during high-productivity times, you will maximize efficiency. And by keeping interruptions to a minimum during high-productivity times, you will get the most from your best hours. We will talk about dealing with interruptions in Part III.

Using Low-Productivity Times

There are many low-priority or routine tasks that can be done during low-productivity times. For example, if you are a morning person, shopping for groceries should be put off until later in the day when your energies are at their lowest.

Your Attention Span

Another biological factor is attention span, the period of time over which we can devote clear and undivided attention to a particular subject.

Children and older people tend to have shorter spans of attention. You will note that children's television programs, such as "Sesame Street," recognizing the child's shorter attention span, tend to put learning into brief segments geared to having the maximum impact in the shortest time.

You may also remember meetings that seemed to drag on forever. Once the length of the meeting has exceeded your attention span, it is likely to feel like forever, even if the time isn't really that long. (Another problem with meetings is that if the subject matter being discussed has no interest or appeal to you, your attention span may disappear completely.)

Changes in Attention Span

Your normal attention span will be longer during your prime biological clock hours and shorter when you are tired or ill. You may be able to lengthen your attention span at times by coffee or other artificial means; but the best policy is to learn your body's normal patterns, get to know them realistically, and plan around them.

6 · CALENDARS

Your calendar is the clearing house for the management of
your time. Use it as an extension of your memory by
writing down appointments, things to do, and ideas to
remember. If you learn only two or three critical tech-
niques from this book, one of them should be the use of the
calendar.

Master Calendar

While we recommend the use of two calendars, a master
calendar and a portable calendar, the master calendar is
by far the more important.

Everyone who wants to get organized and use time to
the best advantage should keep a master calendar. On this
calendar should be registered each appointment as well as
all scheduling deadlines from your "to do" lists for the
week and/or month. And it is from this calendar that your
daily "to do" list is begun.

We recommend using a calendar with lots of writing
space for each day. Everyone has personal preferences in
calendars, but we prefer the type that is desk size and
presents a week at a time. This allows you to see what you
have scheduled for the week and how much time you have
remaining to allocate.

Begin Your Year

You should prepare your master calendar at the beginning
of each year. Write all your periodically recurring events
on the calendar. These include filing your income tax by
April 15; filing quarterly tax returns in April, June, Sep-
tember, and the following January; dentist and doctor appointments; paying the rent or mortgage on the first of
every month; etc.

No Nonsense Calendar Tips

Tip: When you are preparing your new calendar, go over your last year's calendar and mark birthdays and anniversaries or other special days that you don't want to forget.

Tip: Build adequate preparation times into your calendar. Let's say that you mark July 16 on the calendar as your father's birthday. But discovering it on the 16th is a little late. So we suggest that you mark July 10, for example, as "buy birthday present for Dad," July 12 as "buy birthday card for Dad," and July 13 as "mail card to Dad." If you do this with all your recurring tasks, you will never be caught by surprise (as long as you check your calendar every day, which of course is an absolute necessity).

Tip: Note other things you don't want to forget on your calendar—the day the housekeeper comes, the date to change the water filter, the month to have your car inspected, the month of your annual physical, etc.

Portable Calendar

For those of us who do not work at home, a portable calendar for the pocket or purse is indispensable. It can be used in conjunction with, or used as, your daily "to do" list. (See Chapter 4.) All your appointments must be entered on both your master and portable calendars. In this way you will never miss an engagement. Some people now use pocket size computers as portable calendars because they can be programmed to list meetings, appointments, opera tickets, clothing sizes, etc.

You don't have to put every item from your master calendar on your portable one. Rather, your portable calendar should be limited to your daily appointments, your "today" list (see Chapter 4), and selected activity records. For example, you could use your portable calendar to note tax-deductible taxi rides, meals, etc.

Secretary's Calendar

Many people with secretaries find it helpful for their secretary or assistant to keep an identical master calendar (usually, but not necessarily, limited to work-related events) so that he/she can be aware of your activities and help you meet your scheduling demands.

Check in with Your Calendar

Make a habit of checking your calendar the first thing each and every morning, or just before you go to bed. Some people claim that if they go over their next day's schedule just before they retire, their subconscious begins to work out problems while they are asleep. We aren't completely convinced by this, but it seems worth a try. On the other hand, if thinking about tomorrow's problems interferes with your sleep, get up 15 minutes earlier and do your calendar checking in the morning.

Using the Calendar

The calendar not only lets us note when certain tasks have to be finished, but gives us a way of planning out in detail the steps needed for completion.

Here's an example. Let's say that the Sherman report has to be finished by Tuesday, April 20. You received the assignment today, Thursday, April 1. The first thing to do is to put "Sherman report due" on your calendar on April 20.

Now take the Sherman assignment and divide it up into its component parts. How many individual tasks have to be done to complete the report? Here are some examples:

1. Research the present distribution of the Sherman product.
2. Research the competition.
3. Analyze the Sherman price structure vis-à-vis the competition.

4. Draw conclusions and do first draft of report.
5. Revise draft into final report.

Now, you must estimate the time it will take you to complete each phase of the project. Your schedule might look something like this:

1. Research the present distribution of the Sherman product:
   4 days, plus 1 day to visit the Sherman plant = 5 days
2. Research the competition:
   1 day making phone calls, plus 1 on the road = 2 days
3. Analyze the Sherman price structure vis-à-vis the competition:
   1 day
4. Draw conclusions and do first draft of report:
   3 days
5. Revise draft into final report:
   2 days

So you would mark the days on your calendar as follows:

April 1, 2, 5, 6, and 7—research the present distribution of the Sherman product.
April 8 and 9—research the competition.
April 12—analyze the Sherman price structure vis-à-vis the competition.
April 13, 14 and 15—draw conclusions and do first draft of report.
April 16 and 19—revise draft into final report.
April 20—Sherman report completed.

7 · DO IT NOW!

Before we discuss Do It Now!, the final step in the G•O•L•D Principle, let us inspire you with a few traditional sayings:

> He who hesitates is lost.
> There's no time like the present.
> A stitch in time saves nine.
> Nothing ventured, nothing gained.

Do It Now! is the symbol of your ability to take control of your time and your life, set its direction and establish its course.

No matter what the task, you have to begin to Do It! before it can get done. Obvious? Yes—but how many times have you turned away from a difficult or unpleasant task, as if you thought it might disappear or get done by itself in some mysterious way?

So, Do It! And if you do it immediately, you will be far more efficient. If you wait, you will have to reacquaint yourself with the facts before you can handle the task. When we say Do It!, we mean NOW!

8 · GOALS REVISITED

Now that you have worked through the G•O•L•D Principle, it's time to go back, as we promised, and discuss the first step, setting goals, in greater depth. In Chapter 2, we began our work on the G•O•L•D Principle by limiting ourselves to a one-year period. Now is the time to think about your longer-term goals and to begin to map out ways to achieve them.

Long-Term Goals

Begin just as you did when you were setting goals for a year. Start with a clean sheet of paper, a pencil, and absolute quiet. Take the next 10 to 30 minutes, or even longer, to think about your plans, your hopes, your desires, and even your fondest dreams. Think about what means the most to you and what you really want to accomplish during your life. What would you really like to be doing 5, 10, or 20 years from now? Don't hesitate to recognize your own desires, no matter how foolish, difficult, or even impossible they may appear.

After taking the time you need, write your goals down. Note them briefly, without excessive verbiage, and as clearly as possible. Express your goals as much as possible in "action words" that stress what *you* can do.

No Hidden Agendas

We emphasize that when you think about your goals, you must be absolutely honest. Don't hide anything from yourself. If you think it ridiculous to want to be an actor or pilot at your stage in life, yet it is something you really want—write it down as a goal. After you analyze the goal and break it down into its component parts using the G•O•L•D Principle, you may find that it isn't impossible, or perhaps that you can approach it in a different way than the way you have envisioned.

Some Examples

Bob always wanted to be a writer. But in order to support his family, he abandoned his goal and settled for a boring but secure government job. He is now 55 years old and, until recently, faced the rest of his life being sure that he would never achieve his real desire. However, taking the time to think seriously about long-range goals and priorities moved Bob from despair to action. No, he did not quit his secure government job and abandon his excellent retirement plan in order to visit the South Seas and write television scripts about the natives. Instead, he saw that the way to begin to achieve his long-range goal of being a writer, a career that he could begin and continue after retirement, was to work hard at reviving his neglected writing skills. Bob enrolled in an evening creative writing class at a local university and began to prepare for his second career while his first was still in full swing.

Next, consider Sharon, who once wanted to be a painter, but instead married at age 21 and raised three children who are now in college. With the children away, Sharon, now age 48, tried to fill her time with volunteer work, but still felt dissatisfied. After thinking more carefully about her desires and goals, she realized that her fondest wish was to renew her interest in painting. She investigated the art schools in her area, enrolled in an oil painting course, cut down on her volunteer work, and began to spend two afternoons each week visiting art museums to renew her knowledge of art. Most important, she converted her married son's room into a studio and set aside every morning from 9:00 A.M. to 11:30 for painting.

Mid-Range and Shorter Goals

As you can see from the above examples, setting longer-range goals is likely to immediately create new shorter-term goals that are necessary to move toward your long-term objectives. But there are also, as we said earlier, certain mid-range and shorter goals that exist independently for their own sakes.

You should carefully think over, and write down, your mid-range and shorter goals, just as you did for your longer-range goals. Think of the steps needed to reach your longer-term objectives; think also of the goals you want simply for themselves.

For Bob, the would-be writer, mid-range goals include taking courses in creative writing, journalism, and 20th-century literature. Bob has also set himself the ambitious mid-range goal of selling his first short story within the next three years. His shorter-term goals include enrolling in a class that begins within a month, purchasing textbooks, finding a parking place near the school, and exploring nearby restaurants where he can have dinner on school nights.

For Sharon, the born-again painter, mid-range goals include taking art courses and visiting museums. In addition, she and her husband are planning to move from the suburbs to midtown. Their house is too large, now that the children are grown; in midtown, Sharon will be closer to her course and museums, and her husband looks forward to being able to walk to work. So Sharon's mid-range goals also include learning about condominiums and co-ops and finding a new place to live in town. Her short-term goals include selling or giving away the furniture in her son's room, arranging for some of his belongings to be stored, and purchasing art supplies. In addition, she intends to spend some time each day studying the real estate pages and reading co-op and condominium news and advertisements.

Updating Your Goals

One lesson from the above examples is that people's goals can and should change. Sometimes they are changed by circumstance, by outside forces. But changes in your own desires or objectives are just as important, if not more so.

For this reason, we strongly recommend that you reevaluate your goals periodically. How often is up to you. One of your authors takes a bit of quiet time each New Year's Day to rethink and reorganize, and we recommend that you consider doing the same. But once a year, in our experience, is rarely enough, and there are some stages in life when changes come hard and fast. We recommend that you make it a habit to spend a quiet time reconsidering your objectives whenever your situation or ideas have changed in a way that calls for reevaluation.

An Immediate Review

We suggest one step in reevaluation right now. After you have taken the time to think about your longer-term and mid-range goals, go back to the one-year goals with which we began work in Chapter 2. Does the list still satisfy you? Don't be surprised if your near-term goals need revision, as often happens when you have reworked your longer-term objectives. And don't hesitate to take whatever time is needed to rethink and reorganize. Time management can do the most for you only if you make the constant effort to rethink your goals and your priorities.

No Right or Wrong Answers

A few closing thoughts about goals. First, remember that there are no "correct" goals, no right or wrong goals. Only you can determine what will make your life more satisfying and fulfilling over the next 5, 25, or 50 years.

Setting Mutual Goals

Second, consider setting goals with others. We have usually talked as if goals were a purely personal affair, and in many cases that is true. But there are some goals which can be set, and perhaps even should be set, together with others. You may want to set mutual goals together with family, or with those with whom you work. There may be times when you can set mutual goals with friends. The knowledge of mutually shared, consciously established goals often helps people work or live together successfully.

Remember Your Goals

Finally—*remember* your goals, and keep them in mind. Renew them often to keep on the right track.

PART II
COPING WITH PAPER

PART II

9 · TOSS IT!
FILE IT! MOVE IT!

Paper! We receive so much of it each day that learning how to cope with paper deserves its own Part.

Studies have shown that the reason papers pile up is that the recipient of the paper either can't or won't decide what to do with it. This holds true for mail we receive, newspapers and magazines we buy, and papers we generate. You must train yourself to do something positive with each piece of paper. Never just put a piece of paper down. Always make some decision about it. Once again we remind you to Do It Now!

Three Choices

We have developed three No Nonsense rules for coping with paper. They are:

Toss It!
File It!
Move It!

Toss It!

At least 80 percent of the paper we must deal with can be tossed into the trash without ceremony. Be brutal. Most paper is unnecessary, unwanted and basically useless to you. If you don't need it, don't want to file it, and have no one to give it to—toss it, in the trash.

File It!

Much of the mail you get in the office, and some of the mail you get at home, should be filed for further reference. We will talk about setting up a home filing system in Chapter 10.

But most of what you receive can be read and tossed (or tossed without reading). If you don't think you will ever need the piece of paper in the future, don't file it— toss it.

Move It!

This is perhaps our most difficult rule. If the piece of paper represents a task that someone else can handle with greater knowledge or efficiency, move it to them. Even if the task is one which you yourself can do best, consider whether you should shift it to someone else to relieve pressure on your own time. Delegating responsibility extends to the home as well as the workplace. (Of course, if you aren't in a position to delegate authority, you may have to deal with the paper yourself. But even in that case, Move It! applies. You must do something with that paper— don't just let it accumulate dust.)

At home, Move It! may often not be practical. But if your spouse or partner is better at a certain task or at making a certain type of decision, perhaps you can Move It! to him/her. For example, let's say that you receive an impressive-looking information kit on a mutual fund. You know very little about investing, but you know that your spouse has been getting interested in the subject. So you

Move It! to your spouse—remembering to point out, graciously, that the material really should be reviewed by the more knowledgeable person in the household.

The Dots Have It

As an experiment, we'd like you to take this famous time management test.

Every time you receive a piece of paper, put a small dot in the upper right corner. Then every time you handle that piece of paper again, add one more dot. When you have five dots, you *must* do something with the paper. You will be surprised how quickly the dots accumulate and how many times you waste precious seconds handling and rehandling the same piece of paper.

10 · THE ART OF FILING

We think files are the greatest invention since the wheel. A filing system provides easy access to all the pieces of paper we need to keep.

Your filing system should be intelligible to you and to others. Files should usually be arranged alphabetically and cross-referenced for easy access. Additions to individual files should be uniformly placed either at the front or the back of each folder.

Make Enough Files

The first rule is to set up adequate files. If you do the job right, you will probably find that you need more file drawers, more folders, and more labels (if you like labels) than you originally guessed. But it is much better to have too many files (they can always be eliminated) than to let paper accumulate and clutter your room because you don't have the proper place to put it. Take the time to set up adequate files as the need for them arises. Otherwise you will spend far more time shuffling and reshuffling papers for which you have no storage place.

Setting Up Your Files

All offices have filing systems. Why not have a filing system at home to ensure the easy retrieval of important documents?

Home files should be kept together in one place. Below is a sample list of home files:

Bank statements
Bills to pay
Care and cleaning instructions for special products, like specially treated upholstered furniture or rugs

Credit card statements
Health documents
Inoculations
Insurance—automobile
Insurance—health
Insurance—life
Insurance—property
Investments
Paid bills and receipts
Product information
School information
Taxes
Vacation information (interesting places to go, where to stay, etc.)
Warranties and guarantees on appliances and other goods purchased
Will

The above is only a small sample. You will need many more folders reflecting your own activities and interests.

Coding Your Files

Many people code their files for even easier access. Color coding is very popular. We have a friend who uses pink files for everything related to her daughter, blue for her son, and yellow for family matters. You can establish your own coding system, if you think it will be of help.

Tickler Files

Tickler files remind you to do things in the future. You use a tickler file to store documents that must be handled at a later date, or to hold reminders of future events. Your tickler file works in tandem with your calendar. Your calendar shows meetings and other events. The paperwork for these meetings and other backup reminders should be placed in your tickler files. We find it most convenient to keep tickler files handy in our desk.

There are two basic types of tickler files. We recommend using them in combination.

Monthly Tickler

The first is a monthly tickler file. This is a divided file that has 12 compartments, one for each month of the year. When an item comes up that has to be handled in a future month, you put a note to that effect in the appropriate compartment.

For example, say your car has to be inspected every May. You put a note "inspect car" in the May compartment, and once you have completed the current May inspection, you replace the note for the following May. These recurring items should also be listed on your calendar. See Chapter 6.

Let's take another example. Suppose your boss wants you to check with him/her in two months regarding the progress of a specific account. As you gather information in the interim, you would file it in the appropriate month's compartment in preparation for your report. Should your boss forget, your tickler file will alert you to remind him/her.

Daily Tickler

The second type of tickler file is a daily file. This has 31 compartments, one for each day of the month. Used in combination with a monthly file, your efficiency will soar.

When the first day of each month comes along, all the information and papers should be taken out of that month's tickler file and placed in the appropriate places in your daily tickler file. You should also double-check to make sure that any meetings or other relevant dates are noted on your calendar.

You "trace" items up to the appropriate day. Let's say that you need a report from Fred on June 12. You tell Fred about the report on June 1. Knowing how busy Fred is, it seems wise to remind him about the report to make sure that he is working on it. So you trace it up to the 6th, by dropping a note about Fred's report in your compartment marked "6." On the 6th, you give Fred a call, or drop him a memo about the report. Then, on the 12th, you take the "Fred reminder" out of your file, and—hopefully—his report will be ready.

This is an excellent system to use both in the office and at home. You should check the appropriate section of your daily tickler file each morning just after you check your calendar. The items in today's section go immediately into your "today" file.

Specialized Files

In addition to standard alphabetical files and a tickler system, we find that a number of specialized files can be of help. These include files labeled "today," "work in progress," "project," named files for family, subordinates, or superiors, a "mail" file, and "reading" files.

"Today" File

Let's begin with the "today" file. It's an invaluable tool, if used regularly and kept close at hand. This is the type of file you ought to keep in your desk for maximum convenience.

The "today" file contains all the important documents that must be handled today. Many secretaries prepare a daily agenda for their boss as the first page in the "today" file.

All of the items that need immediate attention, plus the output from your daily tickler compartment, should be put in this file. The "today" file is a transient file. Once the item is handled, it is removed from the "today" file and either filed, tossed, or moved.

Remember that anything to be accomplished today should be put in your "today" file. This can be as mundane as the dry cleaning slips to remind you that you are out of clean shirts, or the file on the meeting regarding your most important client.

"Work in Progress" File

Items that you are working on currently, but that are not due today, belong in your "work in progress" file. You should review this file at least weekly, and perhaps even daily, to be sure you are aware of all uncompleted items; and you should tie in the "work in progress" file with your daily tickler by putting reminder notes in the tickler for each approaching "work in progress" deadline.

Project Files

For people with heavy, diverse work loads, the "work in progress" file may be a giant folder or a whole section of a file drawer. Many such people put individual "project" files into their work in progress folder or file section. A project file is a file that you use to hold all the documents pertaining to one particular project or job. And you can break the project down into subdivisions if you wish. For example, if you currently are working on the budget for the Finian Company, you might have the following folders within your 1988 Finian Budget project file, which in turn is in your "work in progress" file:

> 1988 Projected sales revenues
> 1988 Projected operating expenses
> 1987 Sales revenues
> 1987 Operating expenses
> Profit Projections
> Correspondence and memoranda

Superior/Subordinate Files

You should have a file for each person to whom you report and/or who reports to you. This can include family members.

Mail File

If you have a secretary or assistant, you will probably want to have a "mail" file in which the day's correspondence is placed. As you go through the mail, certain items may be put in your tickler file, or there may be an urgent item that belongs in your "today" file. The remaining items that must be moved to another person can be returned in the "mail" file to your secretary for distribution.

Meeting Files

Some people prefer not to include documents required for meetings in their "today" file, but instead have a "meeting" file for that purpose. Others use separate files for each meeting they must attend. We suggest that you put a note in each meeting file listing the separate project files you will want to bring to that meeting.

Reading File

A "reading" file is the place where you put all the articles and other items you want to read after clipping them out of the magazine or newspaper (and throwing out the rest). You can take out your "reading" file during your less-productive hours, or you can take it with you when you anticipate a waiting or traveling period. Some prefer to take selected items from their "reading" file and fold them in their pocket or purse to take out while waiting in the supermarket checkout line. Others prefer to take the entire file and select articles on the spot. (See Chapter 19.)

Clean It Out

It is important to go through your files at least once each year (early January or at tax time are good choices) and to throw out any information, files, or items that are no longer necessary. But remember that some items, such as old insurance policies and tax information, should be kept in case a problem arises.

11 · DEALING WITH PAPER AT THE OFFICE

Interoffice mail, outside mail, memos and other correspondence can be overwhelming. But if you brutally apply the three No Nonsense rules—toss it, file it, or move it—office paper can be managed.

Decide Immediately

The best advice anyone can give regarding office paper, or any other paper, is to make a decision immediately regarding what to do with it. Or, to use the last part of the G·O·L·D Principle, Do It Now! If you should toss it—toss it now. Don't be seduced into holding items which appear interesting but which you know realistically you won't have time to get involved in. If you wait until later, you will waste time by reviewing the same item again before you make the same decision to toss it.

Another good tip is to put all similar papers together and deal with them at once. If you gather all the letters you must answer, you can respond to all of them when you are in a letter-writing mood.

If you want to send an item to someone else—mark your decision right on the paper. Or, if the document is to be preserved, use a paper-clipped note or a "stickie" note to indicate who should receive it and with what instructions.

If you must handle the paper personally, put it in the applicable file and don't forget to put a dot in the top corner every time you handle the paper.

With a Secretary

If you are fortunate enough to have a secretary, one of his/her daily jobs can be to presort your mail before putting it in your "mail" file. You should instruct him/her to divide mail into three categories—items marked personal or confidential that you are to receive unopened, junk mail for your quick perusal and tossing (these can be tossed by your secretary, if you wish), and items that have to be acted upon.

There may be correspondence or other matters that your secretary can handle without your input. For example, letters that get a form reply can be answered, and the letter and reply can be presented to you for signature. (Of course, the best time for you to sign documents would be during your low-productivity period. See Chapter 5.)

If there is a request for a meeting, your secretary can tentatively determine the time and then confirm it with you later, noting it on your calendar.

All mail that you can move gets returned immediately to your secretary for rerouting. You may want to write a note on the top of the page to the next recipient regarding the action that should be taken. Putting the note right on the paper saves your secretary's time because no memo is required. Of course, there will be times when you need to move a piece of paper with lengthy instructions. In that case, put the paper in your "today" file for completion. And remember, before putting it into that other file, to put a dot at the top.

Without a Secretary

If you don't have a secretary, you will have to open and sort your correspondence yourself.

Try to be ruthless. Use dots. Move it, file it, or toss it! The more efficient you are and the more you get done, the more likely it is that some day you will have a secretary to do this for you.

12 · DEALING WITH PAPER AT HOME

There is a surprising amount of paperwork to be dealt with at home. We suggest that every homemaker have a desk—a place where all the paperwork can be handled. The desk should be near the files and convenient to the telephone. That way paperwork, correspondence, phone calls, and the calendar can be handled at one convenient location.

We now turn to the depressing amount of paper that comes into one's home each day. Let's begin with paper we order.

Magazines

Rule No. 1—If you haven't read the magazine in the last six months—don't renew the subscription.

Rule No. 2—Before you renew a subscription, list three good reasons why you want this magazine. If you can't list three, don't renew.

Rule No. 3—When you first receive any magazine, skim it to determine which articles you want to read. If you commute to work, or have bits of wasted time waiting in lines, etc., tear out these articles and put them in your reading file. See Chapter 10.

Rule No. 4—If you haven't finished the magazine before the next one arrives, go through the magazine, tear out the articles that are important to you, put them in your reading file, and toss the rest.

Newspapers

Newspapers can accumulate with surprising speed, and an old newspaper has very little value except as kindling for a fire.

Never accumulate newspapers. *Never.* Read what is

essential and timely in the newspaper each day. Try not to get bogged down reading irrelevant articles. It is better to clip what you want to read and put it in your reading file. See Chapter 10.

If, however, you find that at the end of the week you have several papers accumulated, quickly go through them and clip the important articles and put them in your reading file. You will be surprised how few articles are important enough to survive your scrutiny, once you eliminate the news of the day (which by now is probably stale), the advertisements, and the items which are unimportant to you. By forcing yourself to clip articles, you will also skim the newspaper, absorbing a surprising amount.

Be brutal—newspapers take up space, create a fire hazard, prey on your mind, and produce a feeling of general disorganization that is not conducive to productivity or good time management. For many of us, they are also a tempting distraction; if you are short of time, remember that reading the details of the latest murder or divorce scandal will not bring you the least bit closer to any of your time management objectives.

Mail

As the old refrain stated, "Letters, we get letters, we get stacks and stacks of letters." And now more than ever. At home, we get catalogues, direct mail solicitations, junk, offers that seem (and usually are) too good to be true, bills, important correspondence, and more junk. The main problem is learning to handle all of this paper quickly and efficiently.

Toss It!

The first option is to toss it in the trash. This is the quickest and most efficient way to deal with at least 80 percent of your paper.

Junk Mail

Junk mail gets tossed. You may open it, but don't spend any time reading that stuff—you have better things to do.

Charitable Solicitations

Solicitations get briefly considered and then tossed if you aren't interested in contributing. There are many worthy causes in this world, too many for the average person to support. And once you contribute to one organization, you somehow appear on the mailing list of every cause in the universe. Remember that unless you are a multimillionaire, you can't possibly contribute to all the causes you consider worthy.

So be brutal. Open the letter. You may read the solicitation, but if you don't really want to give any of your valuable charity dollars to it—toss it. If you want to contribute, toss the letter and put the solicitation form and reply envelope in your pile for checks to be written that month. If you are undecided, you can retain the item in your tracer file until you decide whether to contribute. Use dots, and toss the item if you haven't reached a decision in two months.

Direct Mail Solicitations

Every credit card bill we receive seems to be merely a vehicle for a direct mail solicitation. And then there are those separate mailings suggesting that if you order just one bargain magazine subscription, you win millions of dollars.

We don't mind your gambling a little time and a postage stamp on the possibility of becoming a millionaire. And if you were planning to order the magazine anyway, and the price is right, go ahead. But read the fine print; you'll find that you can send in the entry blank on most of these lotteries without buying a thing. Decide quickly, either to purchase something and send in the contest application, send in the application alone (good luck), or toss it now. If you decide to make a purchase, put the item in your pile of bills to be paid.

Catalogues

Catalogues can be entertaining reading. You may consider piling them up for perusal during one of your biological low times, or for fun one evening. Or you can just toss them out. Whatever you do, don't let them accumulate too long.

Notices and Engagements

Notices of meetings that you want to attend, or engagements you have made, need to be noted immediately on your personal calendar, your master calendar, and those of your spouse or guest if you are taking one to the event.

If you don't note it, you may forget it. So take the time to Do It Now!

PART III
DEALING WITH INTERRUPTIONS AND SCHEDULE-BREAKERS

PART III

13 · THE TELEPHONE AND UNINVITED VISITORS

Proper time management means controlling your time. How you maintain control when the unexpected happens is the subject of this part.

An interruption is a divergence from the day you have planned. It may be a welcome break, such as a phone call from an old friend, or an unwelcome one. What is important is how you deal with the interruption.

Because interruptions are unexpected, they have to be handled on the spot. You must make a quick decision regarding the best use of your time. Your decision will depend on a number of things including what you are doing at the time, what you have scheduled for the day, and the length and importance of the interruption.

Remember that the same interruption can be a welcome relief at one time, and a burden at another. Consider the phone call from darling Aunt Eva. If she calls when you are doing the dishes, you may welcome the interruption. If, however, you have only one hour left to finish an important report for your boss, the same phone call can be a nuisance.

Be Honest and Open

The primary point to remember when dealing with interruptions is to be honest about your priorities. You must take your priorities seriously, and you must explain them clearly to others if you expect others to take them seriously and respect them.

The Telephone

Not all interruptions are unexpected. Your friend may call you every day between 9:00 and 9:30 A.M. That is an interruption, but not an unexpected one. If that time becomes inconvenient for you, simply tell your friend that from now on, you would prefer it if he/she would phone between 10:00 and 10:30. An easy solution.

But what of unexpected calls? Our answer must be divided into two—one for those of us who have a secretary, and one for the majority of us who do not.

Your Secretary as First Line of Defense

Your secretary can solve 90 percent of your telephone problems and make the telephone work for you instead of against you. He/she can screen your calls, protect you from unnecessary interruptions when you are in a high-priority/high-productivity mode, tell callers when to phone to meet your convenience, and find out just when the other party will be available for a return call from you. This process will get easier and more efficient as you and your secretary work together over the years.

Obviously, the person who should get through to you at one time of the day may need to be put off at others. Let's say that you have set aside your high-productivity time from 9:00 to 11:30 A.M. for writing and research. Your secretary should be instructed to disturb you only for emergencies (real, not fictional), family calls, or a call from the boss. All others will be told politely that you are "in conference," or unavailable to take the call at that time. Your secretary should ask when it would be convenient for you to return those calls he/she knows you want to return. By setting up a return call time, you have made it clear that the caller is important to you and that you will get back to him/her at a mutually agreeable time.

Running Interference For Yourself

What if you have no secretary? It's much more difficult to screen your own calls, but it can be done, if you do it right.

The first rule is to be cordial. If you care about the person but don't want to take the call at this time, you must make the caller feel that you really do want to speak with him/her but are just so jammed up with a very important project that you can't do it now.

A sample phone call response might sound like this:

I'm really sorry, Aunt Eva, but I can't speak with you right now. I'm very tied up doing x, y, and z. Could I call you back around three this afternoon? Will you be in then? OK, I'll speak to you at three. Bye.

Of course, you had better call Aunt Eva back at 3:00 P.M., or else this scheme will never work again. Put the three o'clock call on your calendar immediately!

Another technique to limit the time spent on the phone is the following:

Hi, Aunt Eva. I really can't spend too much time on the phone now, but I just want to know how you are feeling.
How's Uncle Freddy?

I am really tied up now. Can I call you later tonight and we can chat then? Good. I'll call later. Bye.

Now, you have made Aunt Eva feel good. You have spent a minute talking with her and you have promised to have a lengthier chat later on, when you have more time and when you can possibly save time by doing something else during the call. (See Chapter 19.)

Uninvited Guests

The technique for dealing with uninvited guests is similar to telephone technique. Obviously, it is more difficult to get rid of Aunt Eva when she appears on your doorstep, rather than on the phone. But you might try something like the following:

Aunt Eva! What a surprise! I'm in the middle of a project that I have to finish this afternoon. But come in and sit for twenty minutes. I must take some time to say hello to you. You look wonderful!

Then, at the end of 20 minutes—or perhaps 30—you can say:

Aunt Eva, it's been great seeing you. But if I don't get back to work, I'll really be in trouble. When can we get together again when I'm not so rushed?

When you have a secretary, the technique is easier. Your secretary will screen all visitors for you. In order for this to work, you must not be within view. Otherwise, the visitor may simply march right into your office and make him/herself at home.

Close Your Door

A closed door is your first line of defense and best protection against uninvited guests. It is a barrier that must be crossed. It must be knocked on before one can enter. It tells the world that you want to be alone.

If someone barges in unannounced whom you don't want to see at that moment, the caller will probably ask if you have a minute, or if he/she is disturbing you. Don't hesitate to say yes. Or you may say:

I have only a minute, I'm in the middle of writing the Wilson report and I have to have it finished quickly. Can we handle what you need in a minute or two? If not, let's set a time for us to sit down together. How's three this afternoon?

Put A Note on Your Door

You could put a "do not disturb" note on your door. Let it be known that when the door is closed, and/or when the note is up, that you do not want to be bothered and that you expect your wishes to be honored except in case of a real emergency. You could add that you will be available later—indicate the hour, and note that you would appreciate it if your visitors would wait until then.

14 · COPING WITH EMERGENCIES AND CRISES

Dealing with crises and emergencies is always a problem; especially if you are involved in completing other important matters or if the crisis occurs during high-productivity time committed to other projects.

Balance the Importance

First, you have to analyze the emergency. Is it a real crisis, or a lesser problem in coping that someone else wants you to take off their hands? Second, you have to balance the value of what you are doing against the nature of the emergency.

Once again we remind you of the importance of being honest with your friends, family, and business associates regarding your priorities and your definition of an emergency. You can't expect others to respect your priorities unless you respect those priorities yourself and make them clear to others.

Of course, there are events which always qualify as emergencies—sudden grave illness, accidents, fire, threats of violence, etc. But think back on how many "emergencies" you have been dragged into solving that really weren't emergencies at all.

Coping with True Crises

In a true emergency, all other work must stop and you must deal only with the crisis or emergency.

Reprioritize and Reorganize

You must reprioritize and reorganize. If the boss calls and tells you that your biggest client, Mr. Harrison, has decided to drop by today rather than next Wednesday to discuss his problems, you will undoubtedly have to throw out your old schedule and concentrate on the Harrison emergency.

But if the same crisis occurs periodically, and Mr. Harrison is known for his surprise visits, you should be able to plan ahead so that the next time Harrison changes his schedule, it will be an inconvenience rather than an emergency.

Coping with Questionable Crises

Your secretary will often decide whether a problem is an emergency requiring your immediate attention, or whether it can wait.

It is often effective to ask your caller directly if this really is a crisis that deserves interrupting your busy schedule. You'll be surprised how many times the answer will be no. Honesty and directness are often the best time-savers of all.

15 · MEETINGS

Meetings can absorb appalling quantities of time. This chapter will tell you how to run an efficient, productive, time-effective meeting.

Some meetings are unnecessary. They result from failure to organize and delegate responsibilities effectively. But many meetings are necessary and unavoidable. The trick, very simply, is to avoid distractions and to keep the meeting as short as the situation permits.

Agenda

The first rule for an effective meeting is to have a printed agenda distributed prior to the meeting. This should be done whenever possible. The meeting leader should make it known that all agenda items have to be submitted, preferably in writing, by a given date.

Attendees may or may not be permitted to request additional agenda items once the agenda is distributed, depending on the situation. In the case of a regularly scheduled meeting, the Chair might reasonably refuse to take agenda additions after the agenda is distributed, and rule that all but the greatest emergencies be deferred until the next regularly scheduled meeting.

Set a Time Frame

Put a time limit on each item and try to limit discussion to the allotted time. An overall time limit on the meeting should also be established and strictly adhered to. Don't schedule long meetings unless there's a very good reason.

Start Promptly

Make a habit of starting promptly. A late-starting meeting wastes everyone's time, and delaying the meeting for latecomers only rewards their tardiness. The Chair should begin the meeting promptly even if everyone has not arrived. If the Chair then demands an explanation of every latecomer, it should inspire promptness in the future.

Delegate Responsibility

Your agenda should name the person responsible for leading the discussion on each subject. The Chair may summarize the discussion.

After the matter has been concluded and an action decided upon, an individual should be named to take follow-up responsibility.

Circulation of Agenda and Minutes

It is often the case that someone doesn't need to attend a meeting, or actually can't attend, but needs to be aware of what transpired. In this case, the person should be on the circulation list for the agenda (which will also help the person decide whether or not to attend the meeting). In addition, if there are meeting minutes, this individual should receive a copy, whether or not he/she attended.

A Sample

Here is a sample meeting agenda:

2:00 Discussion of the Felicity report (Sam Burns) (10 minutes)
2:10 Introduction of the Jackson project (Sarah Rose) (10 minutes)
2:20 Delegation of duties regarding Jackson and scheduling reports (Chair) (5 minutes)
2:25 Recap of budget (Chair) (5 minutes)
2:30 Discussion of budget problems (Chair) (20 minutes)
2:50 Delegation of budget responsibilities (Chair) (5 minutes)

2:55 Recap of individual responsibilities on above matters (Chair) (5 minutes)
3:00 Adjourn

PART IV
HOW TO AVOID BEING OVERWHELMED

PART IV

16 · SAYING NO

Learning to say no is one of the hardest lessons in time management. We all want to be agreeable to others; we all want to appear endlessly energetic. Our first response to any request or demand is usually to say yes, even if we are so busy that it makes no sense at all to add another item to our roster.

Requests and Orders

Because the word "demand" is sometimes ambiguous, we will phrase this chapter in terms of requests and orders. On the job, you may receive *orders* about which you have no choice. But more often we receive *requests*, and we do have a choice.

So consider the request. Is it unreasonable? Has

the requester considered *your* situation? Are *you* really the person who should do whatever is being requested? Is the requester trying to unload on you a task that he/she should be doing or that should be delegated to someone else?

Managing the No

If, after considering, you decide to say no, don't let yourself be embarrassed; say it directly and simply, trying not to be defensive or aggressive. If you think the requester deserves an explanation of why you have given priority to other matters, keep it simple and direct; a long, complicated excuse will only make both of you uncomfortable.

For some of us, saying no is difficult and takes practice. One of your authors believes that his life took a major turn for the better when he learned that it was possible to say no to a request honestly, straightforwardly, and without irritation, resentment, or guilt. Learning to say no is part of the process of learning to be honest with other people. It's well worth the effort.

Respect Your Time

We suggested, above, that you question whether other people are considering *your* situation. But are you letting them *know* your situation? If you always say yes, people will naturally assume that you have the time (and inclination) to be helpful whenever someone asks. If you have your own priorities, don't expect other people to guess them; it's up to you to make them clear. If you don't respect your time, and all that you have to do, other people certainly will not respect it.

Take Time to Think

Before you agree to take on a time-consuming commitment, consider your other responsibilities. We suggest that you take at least 24 hours to think it over. Then, if your answer is no, people will feel that you at least gave the matter serious consideration; and if your answer is yes, you will have made clear that it was not an easy decision for you to make.

Saying No at Work

Unfortunately, you may not have the luxury of saying no at work, but there are other ways to avoid being overburdened.

If your boss piles yet another time-consuming project on your shoulders, you can ask him/her precisely what your time priorities should be. Remind your boss that you are also working on several other projects with upcoming deadlines. Ask how this new project fits into your time management scheme. Should you delay completion of another important project in order to complete this one? How should you rank this new project in terms of priority? Involving your boss in setting your time priorities will save you from inadvertently setting incorrect priorities for yourself.

17 · WHEN AND HOW NOT TO BE PERFECT

One problem all of us face is our desire to do every task to the very best of our ability. Yet this isn't always necessary. While many things must be done perfectly, others need only be done reasonably well. An important time management technique is learning that it sometimes doesn't pay to be perfect.

High Payoff/Perfection

As we said in Chapter 4, you must organize your priorities according to a high-payoff/high-priority scale. Use that same scale to judge the degree of perfection required, and consider whether your perfection in one item will cause another, more important project to suffer. Your time is limited—make the extra effort to be perfect only when there's good reason. If you are trying to impress a client, a report that is perfect, right down to the color of the cover, may well be worth the effort. And any mathematical calculation must be done accurately if it is to be worth doing at all. But an interoffice memo may get your point across very satisfactorily without being reworked for literary perfection.

More Examples

Here's a concrete example. You are working on a budget that is due on the president's desk at noon. Your immediate boss, the vice president for sales, phones to ask you for some statistics he needs immediately. You explain that you are in a crisis, wrapping up the budget figures for the president. However, knowing that the vice president needs the statistics now, you tell him that you will have your secretary type them immediately in rough form. You assure him that the statistics will be perfect, but the format may be rough and the language of the transmittal memorandum may not be perfect.

An example at home: a favorite cousin likes to cook and prides herself on the visual beauty of her dishes as well as on their taste. She makes sure that every slice of vegetable in her soup is exactly the same size in width and length. But if she is pressed for time, she abandons her perfectionism, realizing that the soup will taste the same, no matter how uniform the vegetables are.

Are we opposed to perfection? No more than we are opposed to salt and pepper. But as with salt and pepper, you have to know when it is needed and when it is not.

18 · PANIC

Sometimes, when we think we have too much to do and too little time in which to do it—we panic.

Panic wastes time. You can't function efficiently while you are in a panic.

So take a deep breath, and start to reorganize. Do you really have more that must be done today, or this week, than can possibly be done? Or is it only that you have many things to do and don't know where to begin?

If it's the latter problem, slow yourself down and go back to the G•O•L•D Principle. The key, obviously, is to Organize Priorities. List all the tasks that must be done today—which are, in effect, your goals for the day. Now take the time to organize your priorities carefully. Generally speaking, the most important tasks should be placed at the top of the list. But if you are working with others, and you need to complete a relatively minor task to avoid delaying others or keeping them idle, consider that factor also in arranging your list. And if certain tasks have built-in time deadlines, that too must be considered. And wherever possible, break down the more complicated tasks into their component parts.

Finish One Thing Before Starting the Next

Once you have established your priorities and organized your list—Do It Now! Working from the top, do one task at a time, and don't start the second until the first is finished. Avoid distractions mercilessly. If you have a secretary, instruct him/her that you will not take any calls or assignments not related to the day's priorities. If anyone gets through to you by phone or in person for any reason not related to your priority list, state immediately and firmly that you are in the middle of a rush project and will get back to the person at the end of the day, or tomorrow (or next week, if necessary).

You will probably get through the day's assignments successfully. If not, the tasks undone will be those with the lowest priority, and the damage will be minimized.

Taking Time to Gain Time

Panic situations like the above often occur because, feeling terribly short of time, a person is afraid to take the few minutes needed to apply the G•O•L•D Principle and re-organize. Don't make this mistake. The time you take to organize your priorities correctly will come back to you manyfold as the day or the week goes on. It is lack of organization that is the great time waster.

Too Much to Do, Too Little Time

But what if the tasks that "must" be done today, or this week, really are so great that there is no way to complete them within the time period?

This is a harder problem. There is no *perfect* solution; but by applying the G•O•L•D Principle, you can find the *best* solution.

Sometimes your physical reactions get in the way of dealing with a panic situation. Again, don't hesitate to lose a little time in order to gain control of the day. Stroll to another part of your home or office; if necessary, leave and take a brief walk in order to clear your head. If you wish, buy a candy bar or a cup of coffee or anything that helps. Then come back and start to deal with the problem.

Again, you will organize your priorities; but you will apply a slightly different standard. As you consider each task on your list, think not only of its importance, but also of what will happen if it does *not* get done today, or this week. It may be that a major office project can actually be put off until tomorrow, but a relatively minor government filing will cause all sorts of legal problems if it is not done today. Since certain items will have to be eliminated or postponed, be sure to choose those items where the damage will be most manageable. And once your list is complete, start from the top and Do It Now!

This kind of priority setting is difficult. You must be clearheaded and tough-minded, and you may offend certain people by the items you choose to postpone or eliminate. But if you can handle this problem successfully, you are well on your way to being an expert time manager.

Learning from Panic

Effective time management will almost always keep you from getting into a panic situation. But if you do find yourself in such a situation, the most important thing is to *learn from it*, so that you will be wiser and the situation will not happen again.

After you have gotten the problem under control, take time to think *why* it happened. In all probability, you either:

1. Took on too many responsibilities (too many goals); or
2. Failed to organize your priorities effectively (poor planning); or
3. Procrastinated (failure to Do It Now!).

If your problem was that you took on too many responsibilities, then you may have simply accepted assignments without thinking clearly, or you may have specifically underestimated the time that certain tasks would take. In either case, you will have to be tougher-minded next time. When you are setting priorities, carefully estimate the *time* that each task will take, and make sure that the total list can be accomplished in the time you have available, with about a 20 percent margin for error. Almost all of us are at times too optimistic about how long a difficult task will take; don't make that mistake. If you find that your list of tasks (i.e., short-term goals) can't be accomplished in the available time, don't wait until the situation again becomes a crisis—start immediately to shift, delegate, cancel, and postpone.

You won't enjoy canceling or postponing goals that

you consider important, especially if you irritate others in the process. But when you taste the pleasure of getting all your assignments done successfully in the allotted time, without panic, we suspect that you will feel cheerful again.

PART V
TIME WASTERS

PART V

19 · NINE NO NONSENSE TIME WASTERS AND THEIR CURES

If you can identify time wasters, you can minimize them. How many long minutes have you wasted doing something meaningless or waiting for something to happen? Too many? Here are some solutions to nine of the most common time wasters:

1. Waiting

Waiting in line at the bank, grocery store or post office—waiting for a meeting to begin—waiting for a doctor or dentist appointment. Waiting is often unavoidable, but it is definitely a waste of your time.

The cure is to make use of your waiting time. Take your reading file with you if you anticipate a long wait. If the wait will be shorter, take a few clippings or articles from your file and put them in your pocket or purse. In fact, we find it a good idea to keep an article or two handy at all times—you never know when you'll get stuck waiting. If you are waiting at the doctor's office, you may let yourself get separated from your clothes, but you should never part with your reading.

2. Using "In-Between" Time

We all have "in-between" spaces of time—two to five minutes in between appointments or chores. Using this time can be an important time saver.

Use "in-between" time to make appointments, write short notes, prepare lists, read clippings, reorganize, or make a brief phone call.

3. Doing Two Things At Once

Each day all of us do many routine tasks that require only a minimum of concentration. We suggest combining these routine chores and doing two things at once whenever possible.

For example, washing the dishes and/or loading and unloading the dishwasher can be combined with talking on the telephone with your friends or family. Fold the laundry, ride your stationary bicycle, or polish your nails while watching the news on TV. If you're eating lunch alone, pull out a technical article that requires concentration to digest with lunch. These are only a few examples of the many routine tasks that can be combined to save time.

Do you have trouble performing other tasks while talking on the phone? Consider the added convenience of a speakerphone or telephone headset or the kind of shoulder rest that lets you hold an ordinary receiver while leaving your hands free. Any of these will give you mobility so that you can make the bed, prepare dinner, or do the dishes while talking to Aunt Zelda.

4. Using "Off" Hours

Waiting in line (Time Waster #1), even with clippings, is not the best use of your time. If you need to go to the bank or grocery store, try to do so during the noncrowded "off" hours so that you will get in and out quickly.

5. The Search for the . . .

How much time have you wasted searching for your keys, glasses, wallet, or other necessities? Too much? Well, here's the cure.

Have "a place for everything and everything in its place." Each time you enter your home or office, put your keys, wallet, etc. in a particular place—a jar, a drawer, a dish. Make it a habit. Then, when you need them, you know where they are.

Glasses are a bit trickier, since you walk around with them. We suggest having several pairs of glasses, one for each room. They don't have to be the most expensive frames, or the most beautiful style—as long as you have enough to keep one in every room where you might need them. Glasses in the office and the kitchen are necessities. Additional pairs are luxuries that may beome necessities after you are used to them. And by owning extra pairs, you won't have to panic when you occasionally do lose or break a pair.

6. Forgetting to Take Your Lists

We hope we have convinced you to make lists and keep them up to date. But what if you forget to take with you the list you have so carefully made? You will then spend needless time trying to recreate what was on the list.

We suggest a simple trick. Either put your list with your keys and wallet, or attach a small adhesive or magnetic clip to your front door. Put the list on the clip and it will be staring you in the face when you leave.

This same technique can be used for grocery store coupons or other items you don't want to forget. Clip them with your list as you complete them.

7. Running Out of a Necessary

It is irritating to run out of cereal in the morning, but you can always have toast or go out for breakfast. It is worse to run out of toothpaste, soap, deodorant, or another necessary.

We suggest always having at least one spare of each such item in the house, so that you never run out. And when you use that spare, replace it immediately. (See Chapter 21.)

8. Using Travel Time

Commuting can be a waste of time. But it need not be, if you learn to use the time to advantage.

Use your commuting time to learn something. If you can read in the bus or train, take your reading file with you. Or take a book. You will be surprised how quickly you can read an entire book if you commute as little as 20 minutes each way to work.

If reading while traveling is difficult for you, or if you are driving a car, you can listen to tapes and use the travel time to learn a skill or a foreign language.

Finally, you can use your commuting time intentionally to relax and prepare for or unwind from the day.

9. Procrastination

Our final time waster is procrastination. It is such a common problem, and so important, that we decided to devote the next chapter to its causes and cures.

20 · PROCRASTINATION— CAUSES AND CURES

> We haven't the time to take our time.
>
> Eugene Ionesco (1963)

Procrastination means putting off today what you ought to do today. It is not procrastination to put off today what can be done just as well in the future. The latter is called planning. All of us have projects that should be done immediately but that we just can't seem to begin—those that are too distasteful, too complex, or too boring to tackle. So we procrastinate—we put off the work until it may be too late.

Divide and Conquer

The easiest way to avoid procrastination is to divide and conquer.

Every task or project is made up of many smaller tasks. A report may consist of research, analysis, writing, and revising before completion. Making holiday dinner for your entire family entails deciding on a menu, making a grocery list, shopping for food, cooking, setting the table, and cleaning the house.

All tasks can be broken up into component parts. We suggest that you look at a task (especially a difficult task) as an aggregate of many smaller parts, rather than as one huge and possibly intimidating project.

Try to analyze which part or parts of the task you dislike. Which part is keeping you from beginning or completing the project? See if that part can be delegated to someone else, or, if delegation is not possible, look for a way to make that part more palatable.

Do It Now!

The last part of the G•O•L•D Principle applies directly to procrastination. The only way to cure procrastination is to do something about the problem project. Take a small bite out of it—do only one part—but Do It Now!

An Example

You have accumulated $15,000 and have $5,000 sitting in a statement savings account earning 5¼ percent interest a year and $10,000 in a short-term certificate of deposit that earns only a little more. Everyone tells you to invest your money elsewhere, but you dislike finance and can't bring yourself to learn enough about investing to be able to make an intelligent investment decision.

You have been putting off doing something about your finances for the last two years, and now it has become a source of annoyance each time you receive your bank statement and realize that you probably have not invested your money in the most advantageous way. In short, you have become a financial procrastinator.

The first thing to do is to look at the investment task and break it down into its component parts. First you must learn something about the subject. You need to read a book or perhaps attend lectures about investing. Then you need to find a good investment adviser. Finally, you need to take the plunge and make some changes.

After breaking the parts down, you find that you will be able to find an adviser because your best friend has an investment adviser she trusts who will be glad to get you started. And you have no doubt that you will be quick to take action once you know what action to take.

So the real stumbling block seems to be learning about finance—at least enough so that you can talk intelligently to the financial adviser. You can't bear the thought of reading a long, boring financial text, and the financial magazines are too sophisticated for you.

What should you do to break the procrastination problem? First, you could look hard in the bookstores or library for simple, manageable financial texts. Second, you might buy cassette tapes of investment primers that you could listen to while preparing dinner, commuting to work, or exercising. Third, you might purchase a bigger financial text for beginners and discipline yourself to read 20 pages each day until you have read the entire book.

Reward Yourself

Perhaps you will never find finance enjoyable. Then you will probably do better if you structure a reward for yourself every time you complete one of the less desirable tasks. That way you have an incentive to get the job over with and enjoy your reward. The reward can be anything you select—from a candy bar or shopping spree to a movie and dinner.

Do It!

Once again, we remind you that it is all important to take a first step—to begin. The task may not be all that bad once you start. And you will surely be relieved and feel good about yourself once it's finished.

PART VI
ORGANIZING FOR MAXIMUM EFFICIENCY

PART VI

21 · A PLACE FOR EVERYTHING AND EVERYTHING IN ITS PLACE

Organizing your home and office for maximum efficency is an important part of time management. If everything is easily accessible and convenient, you will never have to waste time looking for things you need.

Do Things Where They Should Be Done

You probably wouldn't consider peeling a carrot in your living room, would you? The kitchen, with its garbage can, disposal and sink is a much better place.

Similarly, you should do other activities in the place

best suited to them. Open your mail at your desk, not in the kitchen. If you open it in the kitchen, you will eventually have to take it to your desk—so save the step.

Pack your groceries at the market according to their destination. Put all frozen food in one bag and take it directly to the freezer. Pack all refrigerator items together and all bathroom goods together so that they can be deposited easily at the appropriate place.

Special Places for Special Things

Items you know you must keep, like receipts, warranties, or medical certificates should have a special place for safekeeping. This can be a box or a file (see Chapter 10). For security, put the item in its proper place immediately.

Bank Statements, Tax Receipts, and Other Collectibles

Bank statements, tax receipts, and other important records should be put in a specific place immediately.

One of your authors uses plastic filing boxes, which snap shut and are available in stationery stores for this purpose. Since your author likes color coding, all bank receipts, statements, automatic teller vouchers, and investment statements go in a blue box. All receipts which are relevant for taxes go in a yellow box, and all other receipts (such as for a shirt or appliance) go in a green box. Then, when tax time comes, the preliminary sorting is completed and all that has to be done is to go through the blue and yellow boxes. No more searching for receipts, no more panic. Everything in its place.

Bills

You should keep all of your monthly bills together (in a box, a file, a clip, etc.) and, if possible, pay all of them at once. This will save time and also put you in a better position to understand exactly how much you spend each month.

Remember that the closing dates on your bills will vary. In order to avoid being charged interest, you should check the closing dates and try to find a date in each month when payment will avoid all interest charges. For example, you may find that if you pay all of your bills on the 20th of each month you will avoid all finance charges. Note "pay bills" on the 20th of each month on your master calendar.

When new bills come in, simply put them in your "to be paid" stack; when the 20th comes around, take out your checkbook and pay everything. Of course, you may have a few bills, like the rent or the mortgage, which have to be paid on another specific date. In that case, to avoid confusion, pay only those particular bills on that special date, and mark that date also on your master calendar.

22 · YOUR DESK

Everyone should have a desk or some workplace that is his/her own.

Desk Top

A friend of ours has a sign on his desk that reads "A Clear Desk is the Sign of a Cluttered Mind." We disagree. While you do not need to have a completely clear desk, a desk that is covered with papers (unless you are actively working on a particular project, and the papers are for that project) indicates an unacceptable lack of organization and filing.

One of your authors once worked for a company whose chief operating officer measured an executive's worth by the tidiness and emptiness of his/her desk top. A clear desk, he reasoned, meant that the executive had moved excessive paper to the proper person, that nothing was clogged by the executive's inability to make a decision, and that the executive was doing a good job.

Can Clutter Be Efficient?

Perhaps that judgment doesn't work for everyone, but what is important to remember is that paper clutter cannot be efficient.

True, we all know certain busy people who have piles and piles of paper strewn in a seemingly disorganized fashion everywhere. When asked for a particular piece of paper, such a person magically reaches into the rubble and picks out the precise piece of paper desired. So it would seem that this person has found a system that works for him/her. But does it? Let's take a closer look.

The only way this person was able to locate the precise document desired was that it had been handled by him/her so many times before. If the person were to do the dot test (Chapter 9), he/she would have to recognize that many precious minutes have been wasted touching, reading, re-reading and ruminating over the same problem. A better procedure is to make a decision regarding each piece of paper immediately, and to have a proper filing place for each piece that has to be retained. This will result in quicker action on the problem and a cleaner desk.

In short, try to have on your desk only those items you are actually working on at the moment, plus your calendar and any other immediate reminder lists. Take the time to create appropriate places in your files or elsewhere for the other items that clutter your desk. Do this successfully and your work performance will benefit.

Desk Drawer Files

We recommend choosing a desk with a drawer that holds at least a small number of files. These could include your personal files as well as your "today" and "work in progress" files. (See Chapter 10.)

What follows is our No Nonsense summary of ways to improve your desk and related areas.

12 No Nonsense Desk Organization Tips

1. Don't let paper accumulate. Toss it, Move it, or File it. Use dots.
2. If you don't need it now—get it off your desk. Avoid unnecessary desk clutter.
3. Use drawer files for your "today" and "work in progress" files. See Chapter 10.
4. Use drawer organizers such as a multicompartmented divider, with places for paper clips, tape, pens and pencils, scissors, staple remover, erasers, and other assorted necessities.
5. Have a personal drawer in your office desk for toilet articles to freshen up before evening meetings or entertainment. This drawer can also be used for other personal items such as bankbooks, deposit slips, etc.
6. Keep the things you use regularly nearby. If you spend

a great deal of time using the telephone book, find a place for it in or near your desk.

7. Keep your personal telephone book handy. Make sure that you write all important or frequently called numbers in it.

8. Don't let reference materials accumulate on your desk. Have reference materials handy on shelves or in files. After you have used them, move them off your desk immediately and put them back where they belong.

9. Have a place for your secretary to put things for you, and a place for you to put things for him/her. "In/Out" trays are very useful for this purpose.

10. Take time at the end of every day to clear your desk. This will allow you to review what you accomplished during the day and to plan for tomorrow.

11. At home, have note paper and a pen next to every telephone. That way you can efficiently take notes as you talk and immediately transfer them to your calendar for action.

12. Have a pad and pen near your bed. How many great ideas have you had just before falling asleep that you couldn't remember the next day? If you have a pad and pen handy, you can jot those ideas down and fall asleep with a clear mind.

23 · YOUR KITCHEN

If you have to constantly rummage through kitchen drawers and cabinets searching for particular items, you're wasting valuable time and accomplishing nothing. The time has come to organize your kitchen for maximum efficiency.

In your kitchen, as in your office, the time you take to organize work space and storage space will repay you with time savings many times over.

Here is our No Nonsense summary of ways to organize and improve your kitchen.

15 No Nonsense Kitchen Organizations Tips

1. Kitchen cabinets should be organized so that the items you use most often are the easiest to reach.
2. Use drawer dividers from houseware, kitchen, or stationery store.
3. Separate silverware from gadgets. If you have the space, separate the gadgets according to frequency of use. Put the gadgets you use the most in one drawer and the cherry pitter, butter curler, and lobster cracker in a less-accessible spare drawer.
4. Add kitchen space by installing additional shelving.
5. Add more space by utilizing "undershelves" and half shelves. These removable shelves are wonderful gadgets which you can find in hardware and houseware stores. Undershelves slip under the bottom of existing shelves, creating usable shelf space out of thin air. Half shelves are freestanding shelves that stand on existing shelves. If you have extra space below or above existing shelves, try using these spacesavers.
6. Use your wall space to hang decorative accessories or frequently used objects. Use colored grids on the walls to hang pots, hold spice racks, hang shelves for cookbooks, etc.

7. Use magnets or suction hooks on the side of the refrigerator to hold frequently used gadgets, like the can opener, measuring spoons, or coffee measure.

8. If you don't use an appliance at least once a week, don't waste valuable counter space with it. Store it in a closet.

9. Organize appliances according to use as well as availability of electrical outlets and frequency of operation. For example, if you have a food processor and wash your vegetables before slicing them in it, you should put the processor near the sink.

10. Keep a recipe file. We suggest a 3x5 or 5x7 file box that you can buy in any stationery store. One that snaps shut has the advantage of avoiding a mess if it should fall.

11. Use recipe file separators—indices which divide the recipes by food type to make recipe retrieval easy. Recipes within a category should be alphabetized.

12. In your recipe file, include references to recipes from cookbooks by page. This saves time when you want to make that recipe again.

13. Annotate your recipes to avoid repeated mistakes. For example, if you make a recipe, but think that the next time you would like to add more cinnamon, you should note that fact by the cinnamon ingredient. We also find it helpful to jot a few comments by a recipe so that the next time you want to prepare it, you will remember what you thought of it.

14. Keep a running shopping list. Structure your shopping list according to the layout of your store. If you enter the store at canned goods, and then proceed past poultry to dried beans, try using this layout for your shopping list. And don't forget to bring an item from your reading file (see Chapter 10) so that your time won't be wasted while you wait in the checkout line.

15. Staple items that do not spoil, such as paper products and canned goods, should always be replaced before they run out. Add staple items to your shopping list whenever one is removed from the pantry. That way,

you never have to check if you are low on an item; you will buy it automatically when the supply is reduced.

A Word about Breakfast

Rather than conclude this chapter with comments on grocery shopping, which we frankly find boring, we will close with some thoughts on breakfast, which we find much more interesting.

If your body has to get up before your mind is awake—or if you are an evening person and cannot possibly function before 11:00 A.M., but must be at work by 9:00—you probably have trouble functioning well enough to make breakfast. However, you know that you should eat something, so here's a suggestion.

If coffee is a must, ask to be given one of those coffee pots with an electronic timer on it for Christmas or your next birthday. Some even come equipped with a coffee grinder. Then, every night before you go to bed, you can make the coffee for the next day. And, as a bonus, you will wake up to the smell of freshly brewed coffee each morning.

You might also set the table for breakfast the night before. Decide what to serve, and put all the nonperishables on the counter. Put the correct pot on the stove, have the glass under the juicer, and the cereal out on the counter, next to the bowl. This will cut your breakfast preparation time, leaving you more time for a leisurely and even luxurious breakfast—or more time for sleep, if that is your choice. Either way, you should be a healthier and slightly happier person.

24 · YOUR CLOSETS

Rubble, clutter, and mess are not time efficient. Your closets should be organized so that you can find what you need quickly and easily. Like the executive with too many papers strewn on his/her desk, some of us have closets that even a mother can't love.

Here is our No Nonsense summary of ways to make your closets work better for you.

1. If you live in an area with changing seasons, and if you have enough closets, set up a cold-weather closet and a warm-weather closet. Each should contain only those clothes you wear during that season. In this way, only half of your clothes will be subject to disarray at any one time.

2. Whether you have one closet, two, or more, consider dividing your clothes in each closet by function. Put all of your dress and formal clothes together. Separate your work clothes from your weekend clothes.

3. Save space with gadgets. Use half shelves and under-shelves to create extra shelf space. Use hooks and grids to keep ties, belts, necklaces, and scarves in order.

4. Use shelf dividers and/or containers for specific items (underwear, hose, etc.) for neatness and instant accessibility.

5. Shoes can be hung in specially made containers (shoe bags), put on shelves, in floor containers, or arranged neatly on the floor by color. Keep out-of-season shoes out of the way.

6. To save time in the morning, choose your wardrobe (including underwear, hose, accessories, etc.) for the next day the night before.

7. Apply Do It! to your closets. Return your clothes to their assigned space as you take them off. It's really just as easy to hang or fold a garment as to put it on a chair or drop it on the floor. Do It! immediately and you will save time by not having to do it eventually.

CONCLUSION · BE A TIME MANAGEMENT P*R*O

> Nothing is so dear and precious as time.
> François Rabelais (died 1543)

Can you become an expert time manager? You certainly can, if you follow the principles outlined in this book.

Once you understand the G*O*L*D Principle, you will be well on your way. The G*O*L*D Principle is the basic key to using your time wisely. By analyzing your goals, organizing your priorities, making and updating lists, and Doing It Now!, you will know how to structure your time for greater results and greater rewards.

Of course time management, like any art, takes practice. Applying the G*O*L*D Principle may seem strange at first. You have to learn to develop the habit of regularly reevaluating your goals and priorities. You also have to learn to make the hard decisions that will let you realize those goals and priorities. But as you practice, these steps will become natural to you, and you will find that you are using your time better, and accomplishing more, than ever before.

You will then be a Time Management P*R*O. Of course, you know what it means to be a P*R*O. But in this case, P*R*O also stands for "Priority/Reward Organizer." The person who has mastered the discipline of organizing priorities according to potential reward is indeed a time management P*R*O.

As a P*R*O, you will be able to apply a priority/reward analysis decisively to every activity, every task, every project. As you constantly rethink your priorities, you will quickly recognize the activities with the highest P*R*O rating—those whose accomplishment will bring the highest reward in terms of your own goals. And these activities will immediately move to the top of your priority list and, therefore, carry the highest priority.

Such high-priority items are never tossed or neglected and rarely delegated. Their accomplishment is your personal priority and you will make a habit of doing them *NOW*. Medium P•R•O rated items (those whose rewards may not be as great, but are still substantial) may command your attention, or may be delegated, depending on your time pressures. Low P•R•O rated items, those with the smallest reward potential, should be delegated to others whenever possible; if not, try to find ways in which they can be shortened or even eliminated.

Are you concerned that all this emphasis on efficiency sounds cold and impersonal? Don't be. The purpose of time management is to increase the time you have available to do the things that are really important to you. That's why you set goals. Some goals may be related to career and money, such as working toward a promotion or a raise in salary. But there are other goals which you may consider just as important, or more important, involving your family, friends and other forms of personal fulfillment. Going to your child's school play may rank as high on your priority list as writing an important report. Learning to play the piano may be as important as being promoted from salesperson to sales supervisor.

Being a time management P•R•O gives you the opportunity to realize *all* your important goals—career, personal relationships, and other personal objectives. We all know people who are so disorganized that they never seem to give adequate time to anything. As a P•R•O, you will not throw time away fruitlessly. You will use that most precious of all commodities in ways that mean the most.

So, far from being impersonal, time management will open new opportunities for personal fulfillment, not only by helping you save time but by making you think differently about how that time is used. As a P•R•O, you will concentrate on your goals in a fuller and more meaningful way. By rethinking your goals often and carefully, you will train yourself to keep trivia and distractions under control, and not to forget your basic objectives in life—which for most of us include not only career, but also love and friendship. Keep in mind the memorable words of a song made famous by the movie *Casablanca*:

> You must remember this . . .
> The fundamental things apply,
> As time goes by.
>
> Herman Hupfeld, 1931

INDEX

Attention span, 21

Bills, 88–89

Calendars, 22–25
  checking, 24
  master, 22
  method, 22
  portable, 23
  secretarial, 24
  tips, 23
  using, 24–25
Cleaning, 43
Closets, 96

Decisions, 44

Emergencies and crises, 58–59
  analyzation, 58
  coping, 58, 59
  prioritizing and organizing, 58–59

Filing, 36, 38–49
  catalogues, 49
  charitable solicitations, 48
  cleaning, 43
  coding, 39
  decisions, 44
  direct mail solicitations, 48
  establishment, 38
  at home, 46–49
  junk mail, 48
  magazines, 46
  mail, 43, 47, 48
  meetings, 43
  newspapers, 46–47
  non-secretarial, 45
  notices and engagements, 49
  at the office, 44–45
  project files, 42
  reading, 43
  secretarial, 44
  setting up, 38–49
  specialized files, 41
  superior/subordinate files, 42
  tickler files, 39–40
    daily, 40–41
    monthly, 40
  "today" file, 41–42

tossing it, 47
"work in progress" file, 42

Goals, 3–31
  agendas, hidden, 27–28
  answers, 30
  examples, 6–9, 28
  length, 5
  long-term, 9, 11, 15, 27
  materials, 6–7
  mid-range and shorter goals,
    28–29
  remembering, 31
  review, 30
  setting, 3–4
  mutual goals, 30–31
  reasons, 4
  and time, 5–9
  types, 5–6
  updating, 29–30
  visualization, 13–14

Home
  cleaning, 43
  closets, 96
  filing, 46–49
  kitchen, 93–95
  mail, 43, 47, 48
How to avoid being overwhelmed,
  65–73

Interruptions, 53–62
  defenses, 56–57
  uninvited guests, 56

Kitchen, 93–95

Mail, 43, 47, 48
  direct mail solicitations, 48
  junk mail, 48
Meetings, 60–62
  agenda circulation with minutes,
    61
  agenda sample, 61–62
  delegation of responsibility, 61
  filing, 43
  promptness, 60–61
  setting a time frame, 60

Office
  filing, 44–45
  meetings, 43
  mail, 43, 47, 48
  saying no, 67
  see also Filing; Meetings; Secretary;
    Time Wasters
Organization, 87–99
  bank statements, 88
  bills, 88–89
  closets, 96
  collectible items, 88
  desk, 90–92
  drawer files, 91
  efficient clutter, 90–91
  tips, 91–92
  top, 90
  environment, 87–88
  kitchen, 93–95
  breakfast, 95
  tips, 93–95
  special places, 88
  tax receipts, 88

Panic, 70–73
  learning from, 72–73
  priority completion, 70–71
  solutions, 71–72
  and time, 71
Paper, 35–49
  choices in handling, 35
  filing, 36, 38–49
  management, 37
  moving it, 36–37
  tossing it, 36
Perfection, 68–69
  examples, 68–69
  high payoff, 68
Priorities
  assignment, 11–12
  completion, 70–71
  counting hours, 17–18
  daily, listing, 16–17
  emergency, 58–59
  emotional, 14
  example, 12–13
  goal visualization, 13–14
  listing in order, 15–18
  long-term goals, 11; *see also* Goals
    listing, 15
    monthly, 15
  objectives, 15–16
  potential of, 11
  ranking, 16
  realistic versus unrealistic, 17
  relationship between goals and
    priorities, 10
  rewards, 10–11

  time, 14
  time and location constraints,
    17
Procrastination, 80, 81–83
  example, 82–83
  rewards, 83
  solving, 81–82
Productivity
  high, 20
  low, 20

Reading, 43

Saying no, 65–67
  management, 66
  requests and orders, 65–66
  respect, 66
  thinking, 66–67
  at work, 67
Schedule-breakers, 53–62; *see also*
  Scheduling
Scheduling, 19–21
  attention span, 21
  biological clock
    determination of, 19
    using, 20
  evening, 19–20
  high-productivity time, 20
  low-productivity time, 20
  morning, 19
  see also Schedule-breakers
Secretary
  and use of filing, 44
  use of calendars, 24
  use of telephone, 54–55
  see also Filing

Time management
  and goals, 5–9
  how to be a pro, 97–99
  and panic, 71
Time wasters, 77–83
  cures, 77–80
  doing two things at once, 78
  forgetting lists, 79–80
  procrastination, 80, 81–83
  running out of an item, 80
  searching for something lost, 79
  using in-between time, 78
  using "off" hours, 79
  using travel time, 80
  waiting, 77–78
Telephone, 53–57
  honesty, 54
  running interference, 55–56
  and your secretary, 54–55

About the Authors

PHYLLIS C. KAUFMAN, the originator of the *No Nonsense Guides*, is a Philadelphia attorney and theatrical producer. A graduate of Brandeis University, she was an editor of the law review at Temple University School of Law. She is listed in *Who's Who in American Law*, *Who's Who of American Women*, *Who's Who in Finance and Industry*, and *Foremost Women of the Twentieth Century*.

ARNOLD CORRIGAN, noted financial expert, is the author of *How Your IRA Can Make You a Millionaire* and is a frequent guest on financial talk shows. A senior officer of a large New York investment advisory firm, he holds Bachelor's and Master's degrees in economics from Harvard and has written for *Barron's* and other financial publications.